FRANK THE FROGGY

WHY DID THE FROG CROAK?

MARCY SCHAAF

TITLE: FRANK THE FROGGY: WHY DID THE FROG CROAK?

INTRODUCTION:

WELCOME TO THE DELIGHTFUL AND FUNNY WORLD OF FRANK THE FROGGY! IN THIS CHARMING TALE, MEET FRANK, A LOVABLE FROG WITH A BIG PERSONALITY AND AN EVEN BIGGER SENSE OF HUMOR. ONE STORMY NIGHT, FRANK FINDS HIMSELF SEEKING REFUGE IN A COZY HOUSE, AND THAT'S WHERE THE FUN TRULY BEGINS.

JOIN FRANK AS HE TRIES TO CONVINCE THE KIND LADY OF THE HOUSE TO LET HIM STAY, USING HIS WIT, CHARM, AND A FEW HILARIOUS JOKES. FROM PROPOSING TO BE HER NEW GAY BEST FRIEND TO OFFERING HIS TALENTS AS A TOP-NOTCH COMEDIAN AND AN UNUSUAL COOK, FRANK'S ANTICS WILL HAVE YOU LAUGHING OUT LOUD.

THIS HEARTWARMING STORY SHOWS THE MAGIC OF FRIENDSHIP, THE JOY OF LAUGHTER, AND THE IMPORTANCE OF BEING KIND TO ALL CREATURES, NO MATTER HOW SMALL OR SLIMY THEY MIGHT BE. SO, TURN THE PAGE AND LET THE ADVENTURE OF "FRANK THE FROGGY: WHY DID THE FROG CROAK?" HOP RIGHT INTO YOUR HEART!

DEDICATION:

TO LAURA ANSELMO,

THANK YOU FOR SHARING THE HEARTWARMING STORY OF THE LITTLE FROG WHO FOUND HIS WAY INTO YOUR HOME ON A STORMY DAY. YOUR KINDNESS AND GENTLE SPIRIT IN GUIDING HIM BACK OUTSIDE INSPIRED THIS TALE. MAY YOUR STORY CONTINUE TO BRING SMILES AND SPREAD JOY, JUST AS IT HAS IN THESE PAGES.

WITH GRATITUDE AND ADMIRATION,
YOUR LITTLE SISTER
MARCY SCHAAF

FRANK LOVED HIS POND HOME.

UNTIL, ONE DAY A BIG STORM CAME.

THUNDER BOOMED,
LIGHTNING FLASHED BRIGHTLY.

FRANK HOPPED TO A HOUSE NEARBY.

HE FOUND A COZY DOOR JAM.

PERFECT SPOT!
FRANK THOUGHT, SMILING.

THE RAIN POURED AND WIND HOWLED.

FRANK WAITED PATIENTLY FOR SAFETY.

THE LADY OF THE HOUSE ARRIVED.

SHE OPENED THE DOOR CAREFULLY.

FRANK SEIZED HIS
CHANCE TO HOP INSIDE.

HE FOUND A
WARM CORNER.

THE LADY DIDN'T NOTICE HIM.

FRANK THE FROGGY FELT SAFE

MORNING CAME, THE STORM STOPPED.

THE LADY SPOTTED
FRANK QUICKLY.

HELLO, LITTLE FROG
SHE SAID.

FRANK BLINKED AND
CROAKED SOFTLY.

DON'T WORRY,
SHE ASSURED HIM.

FRANK
JUMPED TO HIS FEET

I CAN BE YOUR
NEW FRIEND!

THE LADY LOOKED SURPRISED
AND CHUCKLED.

I'M GREAT AT TELLING JOKES!

WHY DID THE FROG CROAK?

BECAUSE HE WAS RIBBITING!
HE LAUGHED.

THE LADY LAUGHED, SHAKING HER HEAD.

I CAN BE YOUR GAY BEST FRIEND AND TELL YOU WHAT OUTFITS LOOK GOOD!

EVERYONE NEEDS A FABULOUS FRIEND!

THE LADY LAUGHED HARDER NOW.

O WAIT... I CAN COOK DELICIOUS FLIES!
DO YOU NEED A COOK?

FLY SOUP, FLY PIE, FLY CAKE! SOUNDS GOOD RIGHT?

SHE LAUGHED TILL
HER BELLY HURT.

YOU'RE FUNNY,
BUT OUTSIDE YOU GO.

FRANK SIGHED,
HOPPING TO THE DOOR.

OK NOW...GOODBYE, COMEDIAN, COOK, GAY BEST FRIEND, SHE SHOUTED.

FRANK THE FROGGY WAVED,
AND HOPPING BACK HOME.

THE END!

Books By Schaaf

www.BookBySchaaf.com

Find us at:

9 798869 393104